CCSS **Genre** Folktale

MW01049227

Essential Questio
What makes different animals unique?

The Ballgame
Between the Birds
and the Animals

A Cherokee Folktale

retold by Anna Fenton • illustrated by Sarah Snow

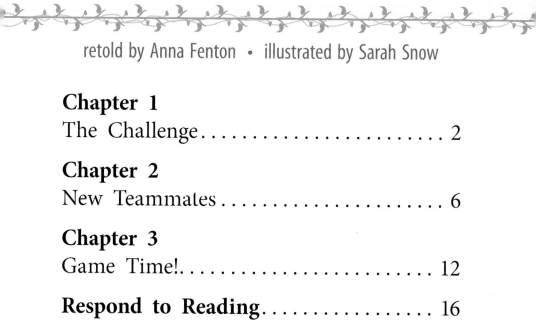

Chapter 1

The Challenge

Once, the four-legged animals challenged the birds to a ballgame. The birds accepted. Both teams danced and pounded on drums. Then the animals gathered on the edge of a large meadow. The birds perched nearby in trees.

There were two poles in the meadow. The animals painted their pole bright colors. The birds covered their pole with fabulous feathers. Each team had to try to hit its own pole with the ball. It had to try to stop the other team from doing the same thing. The team that hit its own pole first would be the winner of the game.

The bear was captain of the animals. "I can push away anything in my way," he roared.

The turtle and the deer were also on the animal team.

"No blow can hurt my hard shell," the turtle declared.

"I am very speedy," the deer announced. "I am faster than any bird."

The eagle was captain of the birds. The hawk and other quick-flying birds were also on this team. The birds were very brave. But they were still a little afraid of the animals. The animals were so much bigger and stronger! The animals kept boasting about how they couldn't possibly lose to the birds.

STOP AND CHECK

How will the game be won?

Chapter 2

New Teammates

The game was about to begin when two strange creatures appeared. They were not much larger than field mice. They climbed the tree that the watchful eagle was sitting in and crept along his branch.

"We want to play in the ballgame," said one of them.

"Can we be on your team?" the other one asked.

"But you both have four legs, not two," said the eagle. "Why haven't you joined the other team? Surely, that's where you belong."

"We offered our help, but the animals made fun of us," said the first creature.

"And they chased us away because we are so small," added the second one.

The eagle felt sorry for the creatures. "Okay," he said. "You can be on our team."

Then the hawk spoke up. "We have forgotten something important," it said. "The little creatures have no wings! How can they join the bird team?"

The birds thought for a long time. Then they came up with an idea. Together, they took the leather skin off their drums. They cut two pieces of leather that were shaped like wings. The birds stretched the pieces of leather as far as they could. Then they joined them to the creature's long, thin arms and legs. This is how the bat came to be.

The birds had no leather left to make wings for the second creature. So the eagle sat on one side of the creature and the hawk sat on the other. Each bird used its beak to pull at the creature's skin. They stretched the skin out from the sides of its body. This is how the flying squirrel came to be.

The birds threw the ball around to test the bat and the flying squirrel. They saw that the creatures could be good members of the bird team. They liked the creatures' enthusiasm.

STOP AND CHECK

How were the bat and the flying squirrel created?

Chapter 3

Game Time!

At last, the signal was given and the game began. From the very start, the flying squirrel grabbed the ball. He carried it high up into a tree. Then he threw it to one of the birds.

The birds kept the ball in the air for a long time. The animals on the ground couldn't reach it. When the ball finally fell to the ground, the deer dashed toward it. But the swallow got there first. He snapped up the ball and tossed it quickly to the bat.

The bat swooped low to the ground. He wove his way in and out of all the animals. The bear lumbered toward the bat. But the bat zipped right by him and smashed the ball against the pole hung with feathers.

The animals stood there in dismay and disbelief. The birds had won the game! It was a splendid day for feathered friends everywhere.

Respond to Reading

Summarize

Summarize what was special about the animals in this story. Use the graphic organizer to help you.

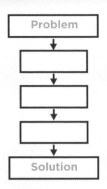

Text Evidence

1. How can you tell that this story is a folktale? Genre

2. What problem does the first creature have? How is it solved?

   Problem and Solution

3. Find the word *speedy* on page 4. What nearby word helps you figure out what *speedy* means? Synonyms

4. Write about the second creature's problem and the birds' solution. Write

   About Reading

Merlin D Tuttle/Photo Researchers/Getty Images

Compare Texts

Read about what makes bats unique.

All About Bats

What do you know about bats? Bats are unique. They are the only mammals in the world that can fly. A mammal is an animal that has fur or hair and feeds milk to its babies.

There are about 1,000 kinds of bats in the world. Some kinds are as big as a small dog. One kind is not much larger than a bumblebee.

The bumblebee bat is the smallest bat in the world.

17

Bats have special features that help them survive. They can fly in dark caves without crashing into things. They make fast, high-pitched

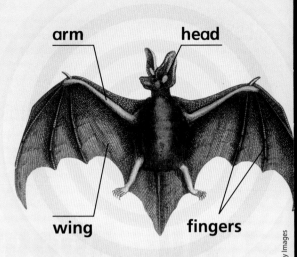

arm   head

wing   fingers

squeaks. When the sounds hit things, they bounce back like echoes. These echoes help bats find and avoid obstacles.

Bats find their way in the dark by listening to the echoes that bounce off objects around them.

Get the Facts about Vampire Bats

Many people are afraid of vampire bats because they feed on blood. But they aren't as scary when you know the facts.

- They're small—often about the same size as an adult's thumb.

- They mostly feed on cows and birds. They make small cuts in the animals' skin. Then they lap up the blood that oozes out.

- They drink about one tablespoon of blood each night. The animals aren't hurt. In fact, they usually sleep through it.

- They are found in Mexico, Central America, and South America.

- It is very unusual for them to bite people.

Make Connections

How does *All About Bats* tell you what makes this animal unique? Essential Question

The creatures in *The Ballgame Between the Birds and the Animals* are not birds. What kind of animals are they? Text to Text

19

Focus on

Folktales A folktale is a story that is passed down over time by word of mouth. Some of the things that happen in folktales can't happen in real life. Some folktales teach a lesson.

Read and Find *The Ballgame Between the Birds and the Animals* is a folktale. The events that take place are not real. Animals cannot talk. Birds did not create bats and flying squirrels. The lesson is that kindness and creative thinking can be rewarded.

Your Turn

Write your own folktale. This can be either your version of an old folktale or a whole new folktale.